# GORILLAS

by Golriz Golkar

**Cody Koala**

An Imprint of Pop!
popbooksonline.com

abdopublishing.com

Published by Pop!, a division of ABDO, PO Box 398166, Minneapolis, Minnesota 55439. Copyright © 2019 by POP, LLC. International copyrights reserved in all countries. No part of this book may be reproduced in any form without written permission from the publisher. Pop!™ is a trademark and logo of POP, LLC.

Printed in the United States of America, North Mankato, Minnesota

042018
092018

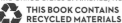
Cover Photo: iStockphoto
Interior Photos: iStockphoto, 1, 5 (top), 5 (bottom left), 5 (bottom right), 15 (top), 15 (bottom right), 19, 21; Shutterstock Images, 6, 7, 8, 11, 12, 15 (bottom left), 16

Editor: Meg Gaertner
Series Designer: Laura Mitchell

Library of Congress Control Number: 2017963429
Publisher's Cataloging-in-Publication Data
Names: Golkar, Golriz, author.
Title: Gorillas / by Golriz Golkar.
Description: Minneapolis, Minnesota : Pop!, 2019. | Series: Rain forest animals | Includes online resources and index.
Identifiers: ISBN 9781532160264 (lib.bdg.) | ISBN 9781532161384 (ebook) |
Subjects: LCSH: Gorilla--Juvenile literature. | Gorilla--Behavior--Juvenile literature. | Rain forest animals--Juvenile literature. | Rain forest animals--Behavior--Juvenile literature.
Classification: DDC 591.736--dc23

# Cody Koala

Pop open this book and you'll find QR codes like this one, loaded with information, so you can learn even more!

Scan this code* and others like it while you read, or visit the website below to make this book pop.

**popbooksonline.com/gorillas**

*Scanning QR codes requires a web-enabled smart device with a QR code reader app and a camera.

# Table of Contents

# Chapter 1

# Great Ape

Gorillas are apes. Unlike monkeys, they have no tail. They go **knuckle walking** on all fours but can stand on two legs. They grab things with their hands and feet.

Watch a video here!

Gorillas have large heads and wrinkled faces. Their fur is mostly black or brown-gray.

Adult **males** called **silverbacks** have silver fur on their backs.

Gorillas are powerful animals. They have long, strong arms and short legs. They can bend branches and guard themselves easily.

A gorilla's upper body is six times stronger than that of an adult person.

# Chapter 2

# The Gentle Giant

Gorillas are smart and gentle. They eat mostly fruits and other plants. They live in groups called **bands** or troops. Silverbacks guard their bands.

Learn more here!

During the day, gorillas nap, play, look for food, and clean each other. At night, they make beds from leaves and branches before they sleep.

# Chapter 3

# The Life of a Gorilla

Mother gorillas have one baby at a time. The baby gorilla rides on its mother's back until it is two or three years old.

**Complete an activity here!**

Young gorillas play and swing on trees. Between ages seven and ten, gorillas leave their families and look for **mates**. They are ready to have their own children.

> Gorillas can live for up to 35 years in the wild.

# Chapter 4

# A Gorilla's Home

Gorillas live in the **rain forests** in Africa. Mountain gorillas live in mountain areas. Lowland gorillas live on lower ground inside rain forests.

Learn more here!

Many gorillas are losing their homes. People are working to protect the rain forests and keep gorillas safe.

# Making Connections

## Text-to-Self

Have you ever seen a gorilla at the zoo? What was it doing?

## Text-to-Text

What other animals have you read about that like to play? How do these different animals play?

## Text-to-World

Many gorillas are losing their homes because of people cutting down rain forests. How do you think people can keep animals safe?

# Glossary

**band** – a group of gorillas.

**knuckle walking** – walking on all fours and on knuckles instead of palms.

**male** – a person or animal of the sex that cannot have babies or lay eggs.

**mate** – an animal that is paired with another animal for having babies.

**rain forest** – a warm, thick forest that receives a lot of rain.

**silverback** – an adult male gorilla.

# Index

## Online Resources

# popbooksonline.com

Thanks for reading this Cody Koala book!

Scan this code* and others like it in this book, or visit the website below to make this book pop!

popbooksonline.com/gorillas

*Scanning QR codes requires a web-enabled smart device with a QR code reader app and a camera.